THE LITTLE BOOK OF GOLF TIPS

PETER FRENCH

THE LITTLE BOOK OF GOLF TIPS

PETER FRENCH

A.
Absolute Press

First published in Great Britain in 2006 by
Absolute Press
Scarborough House, 29 James Street West
Bath BA1 2BT, England
Phone 44 (0) 1225 316013 **Fax** 44 (0) 1225 445836
E-mail info@absolutepress.co.uk
Web www.absolutepress.co.uk

A catalogue record of this book is available from the British Library

ISBN 1904573495
ISBN 13: 9781904573494

Printed and bound in Italy by Lego

'Golf is a day spent in a round
of strenuous idleness'

William Wordsworth

1

To stop yourself lifting your head when putting, force yourself to listen for the ball to drop, instead of watching it go into the hole. A huge number of putts are missed because the player looks up in mid-stroke.

2

Keep your legs still

when pitching.

They should only move with the momentum of your swing.

All the work should be done by your wrists and arms.

3

Make every single shot you play as good as it can be. In other words, concentrate fully on the shot in hand, and **don't dwell on past mistakes.** Easier said than done, but essential if you're going to shoot your best score.

4

Always use your 3-wood rather than your driver

if the tee-shot involves a high degree of risk,

such as a water hazard, very narrow fairway or hard-to-avoid trees. This is part of the important overall strategy for amateurs to play the percentages.

5

Putting is done with the arms, not the wrists.

A simple fix to **avoid the 'wristiness' in putting** that often sends the ball to the right is to move your left thumb (if you're right-handed) anti-clockwise from the top of the shaft to 11 o'clock, or even 10 o'clock.

6

Line and length are not equally important in putting. It is much easier to putt straight than to get the right length. For long putts, imagine a dustbin lid with the hole at the centre, and aim to get your putt within the area of the lid.

7

Evenness is essential to good putting.

Keep the tempo of your putt even

throughout the backswing and the follow through, at the same time making sure that the pressure of your hands is even throughout the stroke.

8

Aim for the back of the hole on short putts. Remembering this very simple advice will help you avoid those awful shots that are left teetering on the brink of the hole but not dropping.

9

For fairway bunkers, take two clubs more than usual (e.g. a 4-iron instead of a 6-iron), use a three-quarter swing, and swing at 70% of your usual speed. These actions should make the appropriate allowance for the fact that you're in sand rather than on grass.

10

If there's one club in your bag **that you almost never use, consider replacing it** with a left-handed (or right-handed if you're left-handed) iron as insurance against finding yourself in a lie where you can't swing from your normal side.

11

When your ball is

in a bad lie, your only priority should be a good contact.

Put all thoughts of distance out of your mind, both in your choice of club and in the actual shot execution.

12

If your lie is on the side of a hill, you should aim right if the ball is above the level of your feet, and left if it is below.

13

It can be very difficult

to estimate the force required for bunker shots. Play sand shots from greenside bunkers with the same force you would use to throw a handful of sand onto the green.

14

When playing from hard sand,

use a pitching wedge and play a normal pitching shot, as though you were playing off grass.

15

For all shots around the green, try lowering your grip by an inch or two. This effectively shortens the club you are using, bringing your hands closer to the ball, and improving your feel for distance.

16

When you play a chip or a pitch,

your hands and wrists should be in front of, not behind, the clubhead at the point of impact.

17

Always play a low running shot

in preference to a chip or pitch if conditions allow. There is a lot less to go wrong with this shot than with a more lofted stroke.

18

When you play a chip shot,

keep your right elbow (if you're right-handed) tucked in close to your side throughout the stroke, including the follow through. This will greatly improve your control of the club, and therefore of the ball.

19

Without being pessimistic, you can expect to make one mistake on each hole. One leading golfer (and Major winner) offers this advice:

make sure your mistake comes late in the hole.

20

If you have trouble lining up your putt,

try this. Mark your ball and then return it to the green with the printed information coinciding with the intended line of the putt.

21

Regain some swing confidence

by using the 'feet together' drill. Keeping your feet together (nearly touching), hit a series of irons off a tee. Start off swinging slowly, but when the 'feel' returns, hit a bit harder and then start hitting them off the ground.

22

Use a reverse-hand (Langer) grip on your putter to

reduce superfluous hand action, and regain control of your putting.

23

Never underestimate the importance of putting. A par round assumes two putts at every hole – 36 shots out of 72, or half of your entire round! A good player will one-putt at least four or five greens in every round, and will three-putt very rarely. **Practise putting as often as you are able** – you will reap rewards in every round you play.

24

Focus on the amount of pressure in your grip. Most amateurs naturally grip the club too tightly –

consciously relax your grip,

and you will have a much better chance of getting power from the wrists, as well as less chance of slicing.

25

Make sure that the Vs that are created between the thumb and forefinger of both hands **point towards your right shoulder** (if you're right-handed).

26

The address is as important as the swing. For middle irons, place your feet at shoulder width. For short irons, narrow this stance by 2 inches. For long irons and woods, extend it by 2 inches.

27

The position of the ball should vary according to the club you are using. It should be in the centre of your stance for short irons, one ball closer to the target side for middle irons, another ball closer for long irons and fairway woods, and three balls left of centre (for the right-hander) for the driver.

28

Balance your weight on the balls of your feet, not on your toes or heels. For middle irons, balance your weight evenly on each foot. For short irons your weight should be divided 60/40 in favour of your target-side foot; for long irons and woods, 60/40 in favour of your back foot.

29

When **addressing the ball, ensure your hands are not too far away from your body.**

For short and middle irons your hands should be a palm's width from your body; for long irons and woods, a palm's length.

30

When addressing the ball, make a conscious effort to **keep your upper body free of tension.**

In particular, relax your shoulders and breathe deeply and steadily – do not let your breathing become shallow.

31

Play conservatively.

Most amateurs drop strokes all the time by playing too aggressively for their level of ability. Aim to keep the ball in play at all times, hitting fairways and greens, rather than going for the pin no matter what the risk.

32

Always get to the course in good time, so that you can go through a full warm-up routine and **arrive at the first tee relaxed and fully prepared.**

If you go straight from the car-park to the first, it will be hard to play your best golf and your round will be compromised from the outset.

33

Spend some of your putting practice time putting at a tee or a coin, rather than the hole. This has two benefits: you don't have the disheartening mental image of the ball missing the hole, and having practised putting at such a tiny target, the hole will seem much bigger.

34

The key to a reliable swing is balance. Your weight should move evenly from 75% on the back foot at the top of the swing, to 90% on the front foot at the end of the follow-through. At the point of impact you should have about 75% of your weight on your front foot.

35

Hit down on the ball. It's vital to understand that the laws of physics dictate that the ball goes up into the air because you hit down on it with a lofted club. Your stroke does not scoop the ball into the air - rather it creates compression and spin on the ball, then decompression as the ball travels up the clubface and into the air.

36

Hooking is caused by a closed clubface at the point of impact; slicing by an open clubface. Pulling and pushing are different faults, caused by a misaligned swing. Note that

clubface position has a bigger influence on direction

than the trajectory of the swing.

37

At the end of your putting practice, before you start your round, hit 15 or 20 one foot putts into the hole, straight and slightly uphill for preference. This has the beneficial effect of helping you to visualize your putts actually going into the hole,

boosting your confidence before you start.

38

Do some basic stretching exercises before you swing a club. This will **improve your mobility and help prevent injury.** Aim to stretch all the major muscle groups, taking care not to stretch past the point of pain, or bouncing to stretch.

39

All putts,

whether one foot or fifty,

should ideally be played at the same tempo.

The longer putt has a longer backswing, but the distance is covered in the same time it takes to make the shorter putt.

40

Develop your own pre-shot routine. It really doesn't matter what is in this routine, and no two players' routines are the same. The point of it is to give yourself a solid base from which to play your shot, a strong psychological zone in which you feel as comfortable and as confident as possible.

41

Be positive in your inner dialogue

with yourself, not negative. This is so much easier said than done, but it's essential to a good round of golf. If you beat yourself up every time you miss a putt or mishit a wood or iron shot, your play will get steadily worse, not better. Monitor the way you talk to yourself, and if it's constantly negative, do something about it.

42

For a lower trajectory off the tee, lean the tee slightly forward. For a higher trajectory, lean it slightly backwards.

43

Remember: **at least 18 of your shots**

– the putts that go in the hole –

are as good as Woods

or Nicklaus **could have played.** There is an element of self-trickery to this, but it will help you to change a negative frame of mind to a positive one, which is essential to good golf.

44

When practising chip shots,

a good exercise is simply to throw the ball at the hole. This helps you to adjust the speed of your arm movement relative to the distance from the hole, and also tells you where the ball needs to land before rolling towards the hole.

45

The importance of having a strong short game

cannot be overemphasised. 70% of all golf shots are played from within 100 feet of the hole. If you could improve your tee shots and fairway shots by, say 25%, or your short game by the same amount, it would be the short game that would yield by far the greater benefit in terms of strokes gained.

46

Practise your pitching around an elevated green. Grip the club slightly lower than for a mid iron shot, and cock your wrists early in the backswing so that the club shaft points to the sky when your hands are just above hip-height. Keep your left arm (if your right-handed) straight, hit the ball square with the club face, and finish your follow-through as low as possible.

47

The downswing of a sand shot has been described as 'striking a match'. If you strike the match too hard, the head breaks off – too soft, and the match won't light. This is a useful analogy to remember **when** you're **trying to gauge the speed of your downswing for bunker play.**

48

Never give up on your round.

Gary Player won three consecutive tournaments in 1978, beginning with the US Masters, coming back from seven, seven and five shots behind going into the last round. So many amateurs can play a reasonable game for nine holes, and then drift or worse on the back nine. Do everything you can to avoid being one of those players.

49

Don't be afraid to use your putter from off the green **in preference to playing a risky chip or pitch shot.**

This is not an admission of failure, but rather a sensible percentage shot.

50

Observe all matters of golf etiquette at all times.

This should go without saying, but sadly this is not always the case. In particular, if you are playing at a club of which you are not a member, check such matters as dress regulations, both on and off the course, cost of green fees, and any local rules concerning prevailing weather conditions, or unusual out-of-bounds areas.

THE LITTLE BOOK OF
BARBECUE
TIPS
ANDREW LANGLEY

THE LITTLE BOOK OF
BEER
TIPS
ANDREW LANGLEY

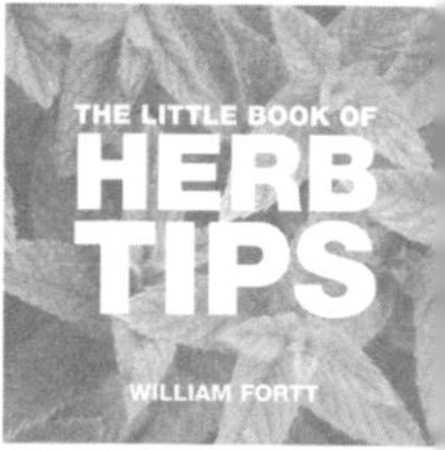
THE LITTLE BOOK OF
HERB
TIPS
WILLIAM FORTT

THE LITTLE BOOK OF
POKER
TIPS

THE LITTLE BOOK OF
GARDENING
TIPS
WILLIAM FORTT

THE LITTLE BOOK OF
CHEFS'
TIPS
RICHARD

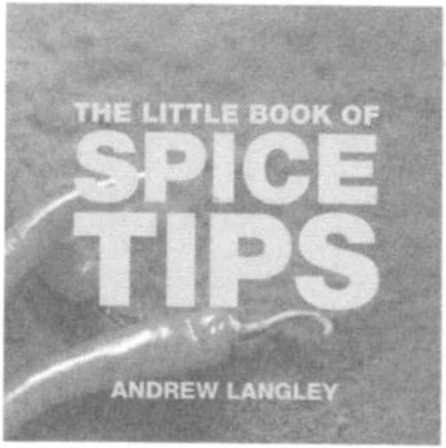
THE LITTLE BOOK OF
SPICE
TIPS
ANDREW LANGLEY

THE LITTLE BOOK OF
GOLF
TIPS
PETER FRENCH

THE LITTLE BOOK OF
TIPS
SERIES